reaching out to

THE PRESBYTERIANS and THE REFORMED

with heart and mind

William J. Whalen

One Liguori Drive
Liguori, Missouri 63057
(314) 464-2500

Imprimi Potest:
John F. Dowd, C.SS.R.
Provincial, St. Louis Province
Redemptorist Fathers

Imprimatur:
+ Edward J. O'Donnell
Vicar General, Archdiocese of St. Louis

ISBN 0-89243-208-X

Table of Contents

1. Power Beyond Their Numbers

"Presbyterianism is no religion for a gentleman," sniffed Charles II in 1660. More than three centuries later, Presbyterianism makes its strongest appeal to gentlemen — and ladies. In many American communities Presbyterian congregations rival Episcopalian parishes in wealth and prestige.

Most of the 4 million American Presbyterians trace their ancestry to Scotch or Scotch-Irish immigrants, although members have also been drawn from English, Dutch, Hungarian, German, and French backgrounds.

Presbyterians exert an influence far out of proportion to their numbers. In the 96th Congress, for example, Presbyterianism was the religious preference of sixty members, including such senators as Baker, Bentsen, Chiles, Pryor, Glenn, Jackson, and Stennis. There were more Roman Catholics in Congress (129), but in the general population Catholics outnumber Presbyterians about twelve to one. Nine Presbyterians were serving as governors in the same time period.

General Dwight Eisenhower delayed joining a Church until he entered political life, and then he became a Presbyterian. His opponent in the 1952 and 1956 elections, Adlai Stevenson, maintained dual membership in Unitarian and Presbyterian Churches.

Eisenhower was the sixth in a roster of Presbyterians in the White House; others were Buchanan, Jackson, Benjamin Harrison, Cleveland, and Wilson. Eisenhower's Secretary of State, John Foster Dulles, who was known as a leading Presbyterian layman, had two children who entered the clergy; one, a daughter, became a Presbyterian minister, and another became a Jesuit priest.

Officially, Ronald Reagan lists his religious persuasion as the Christian Church (Disciples of Christ) which was his mother's faith, but on the several occasions during the year in which he attends church he usually chooses a Presbyterian service. He most often attends the Bel Air Presbyterian Church in California. (Reagan's father was a Roman Catholic, as is the President's older brother.)

Well-known Presbyterians in this country include Chief Justice Warren Burger, David Brinkley, Dean Rusk, Lucille Ball, Dick Van Dyke, Robert McNamara, and Carol Lawrence.

2. *Where They Came From*

CALVIN DICTATES TO AN EXPANDING WORLD

Not only American Presbyterianism but the Dutch Reformed Church, the Church of Scotland, the French Huguenots, and the Reformed Churches of Hungary and Germany owe their origin to a French reformer, John Calvin (1509-1564). Calvin ranks with Luther as a Father of the Reformation, although the two never met.

Calvin did not, as Luther and the Wesleys, seek to reform or revive a Church only to find himself and his followers ousted for his sincere efforts. Calvin joined those who had already separated from the Church of Rome.

Calvin, the Man

Calvin was born in Noyon in Picardy, France, where his father was lay secretary to the Bishop of Noyon. Not much is known of his childhood, but he was sent to Paris to study Latin, philosophy, and theology. In 1528 he gave up plans to study for the priesthood and switched to law. Before 1530 nothing that Calvin wrote or said indicated any particular sympathy for the Reformation.

Yet, in 1533 or 1534 Calvin abandoned Catholicism and embraced the Protestant faith. Sought by the authorities, he fled from town to town, and wrote under pen names for three years. In Basle, Switzerland, he wrote his theological masterpiece, *The Institutes of the Christian Religion.* He was then only twenty-seven years old.

During his travels he came to Geneva and planned to spend the night and move on. He was prevailed upon by Guillaume Farel, a Protestant preacher, to remain and lend help to the Genevan Protestants. In fact, Farel thundered: "If you refuse to devote yourself with us to the work . . . God will condemn you."

The Reformation was well underway in the Swiss cantons by 1536, but Calvin gave it new direction. Geneva became the model city of Calvinism, although Calvin's autocratic and severe methods antagonized so many of the 13,000 citizens that they finally banished both Calvin and Farel. The next three years were spent in exile. Calvin refined his theological system, married a widow, and learned something about handling people. He also worked out the details for his new system of Church government by elders or presbyters.

The Genevans missed the stern but brilliant Calvin and asked him to return in 1541. For twenty-three years Calvin controlled both the religious and civil lives of the city. In the Genevan theocracy citizens were punished for dancing, speaking well of the pope, missing church, or criticizing ministers.

To Geneva came other reformers from throughout Europe. Calvin was intolerant, but so were all the religious leaders of this age; the heretic who could kill the soul was more worthy of death than the murderer of the body. In 1553 the Spanish unitarian Servetus was burned at the stake in Geneva.

The Lutheran theologian Arthur Piepkorn observes:

> Calvin is often perceived to have been an inhuman or semihuman person. While he was an habitual insomniac and a man whose temper, he said, "is naturally inclined to be violent," and while he labored under such physical ailments as asthma, catarrh, migraine, indigestion, pleurisy, calculus, ulcerous hemorrhoids, quartan fever, and tuberculosis, he was not dour or dreary. He wrote and spoke about wine, color, and clothes with appreciation (*Profiles in Belief,* Vol. II).

Plagued by lifelong poor health and driven by overwork, Calvin died at the age of fifty-four. His wife preceded him in death, and his only child died in infancy.

John Knox

One of the men who came to Geneva to sit at Calvin's feet was the ex-priest John Knox. In fact, Knox acclaimed that Geneva was "the most perfect school of Christ that ever was in the earth since the days of the apostles."

Knox had been captured by the French occupiers of Scotland and spent nineteen months as a rower in galley ships. He then spent a dozen years as an exile in England and as pastor of a congregation of English refugees in Geneva.

In 1559 Knox returned to his homeland, where he helped eliminate Catholicism and set up the new Presbyterian faith. On five occasions the Catholic queen, Mary Stuart, confronted Knox, but neither swayed the other. Mary was finally executed by Queen Elizabeth I.

Calvinism in England

Within the Church of England both the Separatists and the Puritans were profoundly influenced by Calvinism. The Separatists had given up on reforming the Anglican Church; they wished to withdraw and start a new Church. The Puritans sought to purify Anglicanism of "popish" practices. They fostered family Bible-reading and prayers, simple church buildings, and a severe Sabbath.

The Puritans dethroned and beheaded Charles I. While in control of the government they called an assembly of Presbyterian clergymen to Westminster to draw up a new confession of faith. The divines began their deliberations in 1643; five years later they produced the Westminster Confession, the Larger and Shorter Catechism, and the directory of worship. In 1660 the Puritan commonwealth was overthrown, and the monarchy and Anglican hierarchy were restored; but the statements produced by the Presbyterian clergymen became the standard of faith for the Scotch, English, and American Presbyterians.

Calvinism in France and the Netherlands

French Protestants known as Huguenots suffered persecution for many decades. The first French congregation was organized in 1555, and a few years later there were enough to hold a synod of the French Reformed Church. Calvin guided the destiny of French Protestantism from Geneva until his death.

By 1571 there were more than 2,150 Protestant churches in France, but a slaughter which began on St. Bartholomew's Day —August 24, 1572—took an estimated 30,000 Huguenot lives. Thousands fled to the Netherlands and other countries. The Edict of Nantes, in 1598, granted toleration; but when the edict was revoked, in 1684, another exodus of Huguenots took place. One Huguenot family which fled France in the late eighteenth century—the Du Ponts—built an industrial empire in the United States. Today, about 600,000 Frenchmen belong to the Reformed Church.

Calvinism won many supporters in the Netherlands, which was originally under Spanish rule. William of Orange became a Calvinist in 1573, and freed the northern Netherlands from Spain. The Dutch Church was disrupted by the modifications of Calvinism proposed by Jacob Arminius, a theology professor; but the synod of Dort reaffirmed classical Calvinism.

English Calvinism in America

A group of Puritans landed in Salem in 1629; most of these immigrants to the New World became Congregationalists, but a few turned to Presbyterianism. Eventually, Congregationalism became the established religion in New England, and Anglicanism held the same favored position in Virginia. Presbyterians preferred to settle in New York, New Jersey, Pennsylvania, Maryland, and Delaware.

The arrival of thousands of Scotch-Irish in the colonies gave Presbyterianism a firm base. (The Scotch-Irish were Irish only in the sense that they came to northern Ireland to settle on land expropriated by the English king from the Irish.)

To a Scotch-Irish minister, Francis Makemie, goes the title

"Father of American Presbyterianism." He organized the first presbytery in Freehold, New Jersey, in 1706. Between then and 1775 more than 500,000 Scotch-Irish entered the colonies. The first Presbyterian General Assembly convened in 1789.

Revivalism disrupted the unity of American Presbyterianism in its infancy. An Old Side and New Side quarreled over the necessity for an educated ministry, but they got together by 1757.

Both Congregationalists and Presbyterians shared a Calvinist theology, if not a Calvinist form of Church government. In 1801 the two denominations formed a Plan of Union whereby mission churches in the West could retain affiliation with both Churches. The Plan probably worked to the advantage of the Presbyterians, but it also precipitated another schism. A group known as the New School liked the Plan of Union with the Congregationalists, but a rival group, the Old School, viewed Congregationalist theology with some suspicion. The two groups split in 1837 and remained apart until 1869.

Dutch Calvinism in America

Just as Calvinists from Scotland, Ireland, and England organized the various Presbyterian Churches in the United States, Calvinists from Holland and Hungary founded Churches with similar theologies and forms of Church government which are known as Reformed.

Holland was itself a refuge for those persecuted because of their religious beliefs; so the Dutch who came to the New World came for economic reasons rather than to seek religious freedom. The first minister arrived in 1628, and in that same year the Dutch Reformed established the Collegiate Church. This is the oldest Protestant congregation in the nation with an uninterrupted ministry.

By the time the English took New Amsterdam in 1664, the Dutch settlers had founded several Reformed congregations. Growth of the Dutch Reformed Church was slow because the Church insisted on using the Dutch language exclusively, and thereby limited its constituency to those of Dutch ancestry. For

150 years the American Church was controlled by the Classis (Presbytery) of Amsterdam which resisted efforts to train ministers in the colonies. Members of the Dutch Reformed Church helped found Queen's College (now Rutgers) so that they could educate their own clergy without sending them on the expensive and dangerous trip to Holland.

Complete independence from the Amsterdam Classis was won in 1792, and a general synod of the American Church was called two years later. This body was known by several names until 1869 when it adopted its present name: the Reformed Church in America.

The Impact of Revivalism and Race

In the early nineteenth century a revival movement swept the western areas, producing another schism in Presbyterian ranks in 1810. The Cumberland presbytery in Kentucky sought to meet the needs of the frontier by ordaining ministers who fell short of the denomination's traditionally high educational standards. It also rejected Calvinist predestination as "fantastic." Many Cumberland Presbyterians rejoined the parent body in 1906, but some did not.

At present, the Cumberland Presbyterian Church reports 96,000 members, mostly in 11 southern states. It operates a seminary and a college in Memphis, and sends missionaries to Japan, Hong Kong, and Colombia.

Like the Baptists and Methodists, the Presbyterians split into northern and southern Churches over the issue of slavery. The southern Presbyterian synods withdrew in 1857 and gained further presbyteries during the Civil War. These southern Presbyterians formed what was known as the Presbyterian Church in the United States.

In 1871, freed blacks formed the Second Cumberland Presbyterian Church in the United States, formerly known as the Colored Cumberland Presbyterian Church. The first synod was organized after the Civil War by black members of the Cumberland Church.

3. *Where They Went*

THE NEW WORLD AND BEYOND

The roots of American Presbyterianism run deep. Of the fifty-five signers of the Declaration of Independence, twelve were Presbyterians. Reverend John Witherspoon, a Presbyterian, was the only clergyman to sign the Declaration. By the time of the American Revolution, Presbyterianism claimed the spiritual allegiance of 20,000 colonists. Hardly any favored George III; the Scotch-Irish who had experienced British persecution in England and Ulster threw their lot with the colonists.

The Frontier and the English Tradition

Insistence on an educated ministry handicapped the Presbyterians in meeting the challenge of the frontier. While hundreds of Baptist and Methodist preachers, equipped with only a Bible, a hymnal, and determination, carried their denominations to the West, only a handful of college- and seminary-educated Presbyterian ministers engaged in such missionary work. As a result, the Baptists and Methodists have far outstripped the Presbyterians in numbers. Also, the Baptists and Methodists made a strong appeal to blacks while the Presbyterians did not.

Schisms and Divisions

Presbyterianism in the United States has had its schisms and divisions. Quarrels between Old School and New School, Old Light and New Light Presbyterians forced Presbyterians to devote considerable energy to theological disputations. In a split precipitated by the question of slavery and the Civil War, the Presbyterians remained divided into northern and southern branches for 122 years. The conflict between Fundamentalists and Modernists began with Presbyterianism and, for a time, also threatened to split the denomination.

Fundamentalism

For several decades after 1910, the northern Church was involved in theological debates. In that year two wealthy Presbyterian laymen published twelve volumes known as *The Fundamentals;* more than three million copies were distributed. The Fundamentalists emphasize five points: the inerrancy of the Bible, the virgin birth, the true divinity of Jesus, the atoning value of his death, and the reality of the Resurrection and the Second Coming of Jesus Christ. William Jennings Bryan and evangelist Billy Sunday, both Presbyterians, lent support to the Fundamentalist cause.

One result of the Fundamentalist-Modernist dispute was the ouster of the popular preacher, Dr. Harry Emerson Fosdick. Although a Baptist minister, he held the pulpit of the First Presbyterian Church in New York City. A favorite target of the Fundamentalists, Dr. Fosdick was invited by the General Assembly to become a Presbyterian or give up his pulpit. He chose the latter course.

Several small schisms took place in the heat of theological battles in the 1930s. Reverend J. Gresham Machen led the protest against alleged modernism in the parent Church. The new Church, organized in 1936, first called itself the Presbyterian Church of America, but court action forced the dissidents to adopt another name: the Orthodox Presbyterian Church. There are about 13,000 members in 95 churches.

Schism and Attrition

One of the early members of the Orthodox Presbyterian Church, Reverend Carl McIntire, began a new Church in 1937. He called it the Bible Presbyterian Church. McIntire's followers differed from Machen on the questions of total abstinence and millenialism.

McIntire extended his protest to the National and World Councils of Churches, which he sees as lost to communism and modernism. He brought together a number of small, fundamentalist Churches into his American and International Councils of Churches. McIntire and his followers haunt meetings of Presbyterians and other Protestants with picket lines, placards, and handbills.

While McIntire and several other ministers withdrew from the original Bible Presbyterian Church and formed another body, the original Church changed its name to the Evangelical Presbyterian Church and merged with another tiny Presbyterian Church in 1956. The resulting Church is known as the Reformed Presbyterian Church-Evangelical Synod, and claims 10,000 members.

These minor schisms have not upset many Presbyterians; they attract few dissidents, and McIntire's antics provide more amusement than distress to Presbyterians. Nevertheless, the northern partner to the 1983 reunion has seen its membership fall by twenty-three percent during the decade which ended in 1980. By the time the decision to end the 122 year split between northern and southern Presbyterians was made, the United Presbyterian Church in the U.S.A. had declined to 2,400,000. The merged Church is called the Presbyterian Church (U.S.A.).

Efforts at Reconciliation

A union of the United Presbyterian Church in the U.S.A., the Presbyterian Church in the United States, and the United Presbyterian Church of North America had been planned for 1958, but the Southerners decided to withdraw three years before this date. The United Presbyterian Church of North America was composed of spiritual descendants of strict Scotch Calvinists. At one time they opposed secret societies, open communion, and the singing of anything but psalms in worship. This Church had a membership of about 250,000 at the time of the 1958 merger. The Presbyterian Church in the U.S.A. added "United" to its official name after the merger with the United Presbyterian Church of North America.

The move to reunite northern and southern Presbyterians was complicated by the civil rights movement, the more conservative stance of the Church in the South, and the revised confession of faith adopted by the northern Church.

The Dutch Reformed Tradition

A new wave of Dutch immigrants started in the middle of the nineteenth century; sometimes entire congregations migrated from the Netherlands to the Middle West. Holland, Michigan, became one center for the Church, and other Dutch immigrants settled in Iowa.

Disagreements over points of Calvinist theology and the policy of allowing membership in secret societies led some members of the Reformed Church to break away at about the same time. The dissidents first called their Church the True Dutch Church, but this was changed to the Holland Reformed Church and then the True Dutch Reformed Church and again the Holland Christian Reformed Church in America. Its present name, the Christian Reformed Church, was adopted in 1890.

The Christian Reformed Church reports 213,000 members and maintains headquarters in Grand Rapids, Michigan. Members of the Church maintain one of the largest Protestant parochial school systems in the country. Besides more than 150 elementary and high schools, the Church operates Calvin College and seminary, two junior colleges, eighteen homes for the aged, and a publishing house. Despite its strong Dutch orientation, the Christian Reformed Church actively seeks converts among the Navajo and Zuni Indians, Hispanics, blacks, and Chinese-Americans.

Smaller Calvinist bodies of Dutch background include the Protestant Reformed Churches in America, the Netherlands Reformed Congregations, and the Reformed Church in the United States. Together these three bodies enroll about 9,000 adherents.

The Hungarian Reformed Church

Large-scale immigrations to America from Hungary began after 1880; most of these Hungarians were Roman Catholics or freethinkers, but some were Reformed. After 1904 the Reformed Church of Hungary began active missionary work among these Hungarians. They formed congregations affiliated with the mother church in Europe, but World War I and the disintegration of the Austro-Hungarian Empire severed these ties.

A Free Magyar Reformed Church in America was formed in 1924 and changed its name, in 1958, to the Hungarian Reformed Church in America. Some 11,000 members belong to 29 congregations in 10 states and several other congregations in Canada.

Altogether, about 700,000 Americans belong to these various Reformed Churches. Although most of the members come from Dutch and Hungarian backgrounds, missionary efforts have won converts from other ethnic groups.

Global Perspective

More than 5 million Presbyterian and Reformed Church members live in North America. About one-half of the Presbyterians in Canada joined the United Church of Canada in 1925; the new Church included Methodists and Congregationalists. The remaining Canadian Presbyterians formed the Presbyterian Church of Canada (200,000 members).

The Church of Scotland claims most of the 1,300,000 Presbyterians in Scotland. The Queen of England, head of the Anglican Church of England, becomes head of the Presbyterian Church of Scotland when she crosses the border between England and Scotland. There are only 70,000 Presbyterians in England. A plan to merge the Church of England, the Presbyterian Church in England, the Church of Scotland (Presbyterian), and the Episcopal Church in Scotland floundered a few years ago.

In Switzerland about half the population belongs to the Reformed Church. Calvinism attracted converts in the Rhine area, but Calvinism was all but absorbed by Lutheranism in Germany. It did better in Hungary, however, where a minority of 2 million profess the Reformed faith.

Dutch settlers took the Reformed faith to South Africa. The powerful Dutch Reformed Church reports 340,000 members in South Africa, where it has embraced the racial plan of apartheid. The smaller Presbyterian Church of South Africa was established by Scotch immigrants and has about 20,000 communicants. There are separate Reformed Churches for blacks.

Presbyterianism has taken root in two Asian nations. An estimated 2,500,000 belong to Presbyterian Churches in Indonesia and 1 million in South Korea. The Reverend Sun Myung Moon, founder of the Unification Church or "Moonies," was excommunicated from a Presbyterian Church in Korea for his unorthodox beliefs.

Presbyterianism was planted in Australia and New Zealand by settlers from the British Isles. Several hundred thousand people belong to Presbyterian Churches there.

4. What They Brought with Them

THE HERITAGE OF AN AUTOCRATIC THEOLOGIAN

Calvin sought to emphasize the sovereignty of God. God was all; and man, unredeemed, was a worm. In his mysterious ways God had, from all eternity, chosen some men to enjoy heaven and had damned others to spend an eternity in hell. Jesus, his Son, had died for the elect who were destined for heaven. Yet, since the fall in the Garden of Eden, man was totally depraved and could do nothing to earn his salvation. The elect would be saved by grace; and, once saved, would persevere until death.

The Core Doctrine

The Westminster Confession presented an unadulterated version of Calvinistic predestination:

> By the decree of God, for the manifestation of His glory, some men and angels are predestined unto everlasting life, and others foreordained to everlasting death.
>
> The rest of mankind, God was pleased . . . to pass by, and to ordain them to dishonor and wrath for their sin, to the praise of His glorious justice. . . .

These angels and men, thus predestined and foreordained, are particularly and unchangeably designed; and their number is so certain and definite that it cannot be either increased or diminished.

Elaboration of a Vision

By the time the doctrine of predestination had been transplanted to eighteenth-century America, it had taken on gruesome elaboration. The popular Calvinist preacher Jonathan Edwards declared in a sermon in 1741: "The God that holds you over the pit of hell, much as one holds a spider, or some loathsome insect, over the fire, abhors you and is dreadfully provoked; His wrath towards you burns like fire; He looks upon you as worthy of nothing but to be cast into the fire; He is of purer eyes than to bear to have you in His sight; you are ten thousand times so abominable in His eyes, as the most hateful and venomous serpent is in ours."

Edwards also reported that "Hell is paved with the skulls of unbaptized children."

Authority of the Bible

Where Luther acted on the principle that what the Bible does not condemn can remain, Calvin insisted that what the Bible does not command must be abolished. In Lutheranism the ritual, vestments, art, and music of the older Catholic tradition were often retained. Calvinism stripped the churches of sculpture, painting, and stained glass. Singing was restricted to the psalms. Lutherans and Calvinists also differed on questions of Church government, the Lord's Supper, and predestination.

Views on the Church

To Calvin the Church was both visible and invisible. The invisible Church was composed of the elect, and its membership was known only to God. The visible Church could be identified by three marks. It preached the pure gospel (of the Reformation), administered the sacraments of Baptism and the Lord's Supper, and disciplined sinners.

Church Organization

Calvin provided not only a theological and liturgical pattern for his followers but a particular form of Church government, known as presbyterial. This polity took its name from the Greek word for elder — *presbuteros.* Presbyterial polity vests religious authority in groups of Christians who represent a number of congregations rather than in bishops (episcopal polity) or in local congregations (congregational polity).

The form of Church government has remained essentially unchanged for centuries. Each local congregation elects a "session" (council) which supervises the congregation. The pastor is known as the teaching elder while the laymen are the ruling elders. Deacons are charged with the care of the poor and the temporal affairs of the Church.

Several congregations in an area make up a presbytery. The presbytery is empowered to ordain ministers, discipline members, and carry out Church business. All the presbyteries in a specific area, such as a state, constitute a synod and the synods form the General Assembly of the Church. At every level of Presbyterian organization, at least half the delegates must be laymen.

Order and Discipline

Presbyterianism in the eighteenth and nineteenth centuries prescribed a strict code for the elect. The elders of the congregation formed a court to examine the morals of members and possibly recommend excommunication for backsliders. Forbidden were drinking, dancing, gambling, card-playing, and any kind of immodesty. Pastors kept close watch on their parishioners and provided "tokens" to those who could qualify for Communion four times a year. Sermons were long and scholarly.

Marriage, Divorce, and Birth Control

The *Book of Order* states: "Ordained ministers of this Church have the right and responsibility of deciding under the Book of

Confessions and the Form of Government which persons they will unite in holy marriage." It adds: "Ministers who are requested to remarry divorced persons shall ascertain whether there is penitence for past sin and failure, and intention to enter, with the help of God and through his Church, into a marriage of love, honor, forebearance, and loyalty, which will continue as long as both shall live." The presbytery must approve marriages of people who want to remarry less than a year after their divorce decree. The Church encourages birth control.

5. *What They're Like Today*

TRUE TO THEIR DEEPEST ROOTS

American Presbyterianism offers its adherents an educated ministry, dignified worship, social prestige, ample opportunities for Christian service, full participation in ecumenical agencies, and an ethical standard which has enabled Calvinist communities to prosper for hundreds of years. Its form of government closely parallels that of the United States and no doubt provided a model for the fathers of the nation.

Presbyterianism's appeal to Americans of lower economic and social class and to blacks is slight. Presbyterians are notably cool toward the aggressive evangelistic efforts which have won millions of converts to the Southern Baptist, Assemblies of God, and Pentecostal denominations.

For many decades after the American Revolution the number of Presbyterians grew much faster than the general population. At one time there were more Presbyterians in the United States than members of any other denomination. Today only one American out of forty-five would identify with a Presbyterian or Reformed Church.

Membership Decline

The membership decline during the past fifteen years has been dramatic. During one decade the northern Presbyterians lost almost twenty-five percent of their adherents. The reasons are many. Some people objected to new confessions of faith; others may have left because the changes came too late.

Some opposed social programs sponsored or supported by the national headquarters; some looked for a more personal and experiential faith in other Churches. Despite substantial membership losses since 1970, Presbyterians comprise one of the largest Protestant families after the Baptists, Methodists, and Lutherans.

The stern doctrine that God elects some to salvation and damns others to hell finds few proponents in contemporary Presbyterianism. The northern Presbyterians modified the classical doctrine of predestination in 1903:

> Concerning those who perish the doctrine of God's eternal decree is held in harmony with the doctrine that God desires not the death of any sinner, but has provided in Christ a salvation sufficient for all. . . . Men are fully responsible for their treatment of God's gracious offer. . . . His decree hinders no man from accepting that offer. . . . No man is condemned except on the ground of his sin.

Controversy surrounded the proposal to adopt a new confession to supplement the Westminster Confession of 1647. The new confession rejects a literal interpretation of the Bible and urges the application of literary and historical scholarship to Scripture study. The document also disclaims the original Calvinist doctrine of predestination, and affirms that salvation occurs when divine love heals the conflicts that separate a man from God.

Until 1967 Presbyterian ministers had to "receive and adopt" the Westminster Confession and Catechisms. Since then they must only promise to be "instructed" and "continually guided" by the various Presbyterian creeds and confessions.

Ecumenism

The Presbyterian Church (U.S.A.) belongs to the National and World Councils of Churches. Dr. Eugene Carson Blake, former general secretary of the World Council, once served as Stated Clerk of the United Presbyterian Church of the U.S.A. Professor Robert McAfee Brown attended sessions of the Second Vatican Council as a Presbyterian observer and has written extensively on ecumenical relations.

The Northern Presbyterians

Always promoters of an educated ministry and laity, the northern Presbyterians support fifty-two colleges and universities, including Occidental, Lake Forest, Millikin, Macalester, Tulsa, Wooster, Muskingum, Grove City, Lafayette, Westminster, and Trinity. Many other colleges have severed church ties. Presbyterians founded the College of New Jersey, now known as Princeton, as well as eight other universities which are now state-supported. Ministers are trained at seven Presbyterian seminaries, including Princeton and McCormick, and at interdenominational seminaries, such as Union Theological. Although the Presbyterian Church usually finds itself labeled as one of the more liberal Protestant denominations, all but a handful of the best-known Presbyterian pastors in New England were educated at Gordon-Conwell Theological Seminary, an institution firmly rooted in the evangelical tradition. Women have been ordained ministers since 1956.

The northern Presbyterians have been supporting 1,148 overseas missionaries. They have cultivated close relations with such independent Churches as the Presbyterian Church in Korea (315,000 members), the Presbyterian Church of Brazil (135,000), the United Presbyterian Church of Pakistan (55,000), and the Presbyterian Church of Formosa (65,000).

The Southern Presbyterians

At the time of the 1983 reunion, the southern Presbyterians counted 815,000 members in about 4,000 congregations. They educated candidates for the ministry in four seminaries and maintained fifteen affiliated colleges, including Davidson, Southwestern at Memphis, and Stillman. More than 520 missionaries labor in Mexico, Ecuador, Brazil, Taiwan, Korea, Japan, Portugal, Iraq, and the Congo.

The Reformed Church

In 1983 the Reformed Church in America reported 345,000 members in more than 900 congregations. Dr. Norman Vincent Peale, author of the *Power of Positive Thinking,* serves the Marble Collegiate Church in New York City. He was educated and ordained as a Methodist minister before taking the Reformed Church pulpit. Another well-known minister of the Reformed Church is TV evangelist Dr. Robert Schuller, pastor of the huge Garden Grove Community Church (the Crystal Cathedral) in California. An estimated 2,500,000 people watch Dr. Schuller's weekly televised worship service. He is the only TV evangelist from a mainline denomination with a weekly program and national audience; all the others come from Fundamentalist and Pentecostal backgrounds.

Reversing a previous stand, which emphasized the right of the woman to decide for or against having an abortion, the Reformed Church in 1983 adopted a resolution opposing "the use of legal abortion in all but very exceptional circumstances." At the same synod meeting it reaffirmed its support of the National and World Councils of Churches despite criticism of these bodies by some members.

The Reformed Church supports missionaries in the Philippines, West Pakistan, Lebanon, Taiwan, India, Hong Kong, Japan, and Africa. Home missionaries work among Chinese-Americans, Jews, Italian-Americans, mountain people, Indians, migrant workers, and blacks. The Reformed Church in America maintains three colleges and two seminaries.

Christian Reformed ministers still wage an aggressive campaign against Freemasonry and other lodges (see page 16); members of this Church cannot join a secret society without forfeiting Church membership. The Church does not abide by the modifications of Calvinism common in Presbyterian and Reformed Churches. Unlike the Reformed Church which belongs to the National and World Councils of Churches, the Christian Reformed Church has been cool toward the ecumenical movement. Its parochial schools, however, often enroll children from Presbyterian or Reformed families.

From a Catholic Point of View

A Catholic will observe far less variety in income and national origin in the typical Presbyterian congregation than in the Catholic parish. Most Presbyterians in this country trace their ancestry to Scotch, Scotch-Irish, or English roots while Catholics come from Irish, Polish, German, Italian, French, Slavic, Hispanic, and a dozen other backgrounds.

Unlike the Baptists and Methodists, the Presbyterians did not lead the fight for Prohibition nor have they made total abstinence the test of Christian fellowship. A Presbyterian is unlikely to be scandalized if a Catholic — or Lutheran or Episcopalian — drinks a bottle of beer or enjoys a martini.

On the other hand, the liberal attitude toward, say, abortion or divorce, contrasts with the traditional Roman Catholic position and that of more conservative Protestant groups such as the Southern Baptists or Missouri Synod Lutherans. On questions of peace and justice, the position of the national Presbyterian bodies usually corresponds to that of the American Catholic bishops. In fact, the bishops' recent pastoral letter on peace has been distributed widely among Presbyterian congregations.

The liturgical revival which has influenced most Protestant Churches has not bypassed Presbyterianism. Calvin advocated weekly Communion services; but, until recently, quarterly Communion was the rule in American congregations. Now some churches have scheduled Communion once a month. Presbyterian churches have been enhanced by stained glass, altars, candles, and crosses.

Communion

Under certain conditions Christians who are not Roman Catholics may receive Communion in the Catholic Church. One of these conditions is that the recipient believe in the Real Presence of Christ in the Eucharist. Many Episcopalians and Lutherans can meet this condition, but it would be difficult for a member of a Presbyterian or Reformed Church to acknowledge that he or she believes what Catholics believe about the Eucharist. The Presbyterian position on Holy Communion is closer to the Catholic belief than to that of the Baptists or Disciples of Christ, but it does not extend to an affirmation of what most Christians understand as the Real Presence.

Current Trends

Presbyterianism has shown itself to be open to new ideas in theology, liturgy, Scripture, and social action. Whether John Calvin would recognize American Presbyterianism as the faithful representation of Geneva Calvinism is not nearly as important to modern Presbyterians as whether Jesus Christ would recognize Presbyterians today as faithful followers.

6. *Where Do You Go from Here?*

Today some Catholic Christians seem almost to flaunt a folksy sense of intimacy with God. Religious values — that men died for in the past — seem in danger of trivialization. And the impact of a revitalized sense of God's mercy seems, for all practical purposes, to have rendered His Justice a thing of the past. At such a time, it may be providential that the tradition of a separated Church, Calvinism, still projects, as its dominant theme, God's sovereign majesty. And that it does; in every phase of its doctrine, worship, and Church polity.

At such a time, it is good that more and more rank-and-file Christians of both traditions are putting aside the vestiges of centuries-old animosity and finding in each others' distinct, faith-formed outlooks a valuable leaven to traditions in danger of being warped by isolation. In increasing numbers, indeed, couples are bringing these complementary visions into lives of Christian intimacy in the marital state. They find themselves called to do this regardless of painfully apparent institutionalized barriers still in place between their faith-support communities.

Such couples often find themselves at odds with the set policies of their Churches in the witness of their everyday lives or with the practices of their local officials. Sometimes, as a result of the ensuing battles, one or both spouses find themselves estranged from the communities through which the gift of faith came to them and through which it should be nourished.

What can such couples do? Contrary to the opinion of some, it is best that both members in such an interfaith union become more deeply involved with heart and mind in their respective Churches and more conversant with the wealth of their divergent traditions.

Such a practice need anticipate no compromise, no demeaning or conscience-disturbing admission, in practice or otherwise, that the doctrine of either Church is lacking in fullness. It will rather give expression to a simple and humble admission that the development of faith of the Christians engaged in dialogue is in progress, and a consequent eagerness on the part of both to share with each other the growth in faith that each gratefully accepts as gift.

In this sharing, interfaith couples should find reassurance in the words of Bishop J. Francis Stafford to the world synod of Catholic bishops in 1980, in which he referred to interfaith marriages as "a special opportunity for Christian growth." He insists that such couples not be led "to ignore the real differences which exist in their faith orientation" but be encouraged to "search out and amplify areas of communality, truths on which they discover agreement and expressions of piety which bring both to a deeper awareness of God." The spokesman for the American bishops goes on to say, "What is behind this strategy is a belief in the authenticity of both faith orientations, if held in good conscience, and a hope that from their combination in the conjugal love, there will result a deeper marital union."

It goes without saying, of course, that if the non-Catholic partner feels called in his or her faith growth to join the Catholic Church, the Catholic partner will in no manner discourage him or her in this. This also is the intent of the Council fathers' respectful statement on *Religious Liberty* (3), "He is bound to follow this conscience faithfully in all his activity so that he may come to God, who is his last end. Therefore he must not be forced to act contrary to his conscience. Nor must he be prevented from acting according to his conscience, especially in religious matters."

We hope and pray that this booklet will help interfaith couples share the vision of faith. The absence of any kind of "discussion starters" is not an oversight; we felt that it would be presumptive, in matters so personal, to formulate the gifts that intimacy urges you to share.

Further Reading

Hesselink, I. John, *On Being Reformed.* Ann Arbor, Michigan, Servant Books, 1983.

Lawless, Richard M., *When Love Unites the Church.* St. Meinrad, Indiana, Abbey Press, 1982.

Loetcher, Lefferts A., *The Broadening Church: A Study of Theological Issues in the Presbyterian Church Since 1869.* Philadelphia, University of Pennsylvania Press, 1954.

______, *A Brief History of the Presbyterians.* Philadelphia, Westminster Press, 1958.

Mackinnon, James, *Calvin and the Reformation.* New York, Russell and Russell, 1962.

McNeill, John T., *The History and Character of Calvinism.* New York, Oxford University Press, 1967.

Osterhaven, M. Eugene, *The Faith of the Church: A Reformed Perspective on Its Historical Development.* Grand Rapids, Michigan, Eerdmans, 1982.

Slosser, Gaius J., ed., *They Seek a Country: The American Presbyterians.* New York, Macmillan, 1955.

Wendell, Francois, *Calvin.* New York, Harper & Row, 1963.

REACHING OUT WITH HEART AND MIND

A series of booklets that explore the history, beliefs, and traditions of the larger Christian Churches in the United States. $1.50 each.

Other booklets in this series from Liguori Publications include:

Reaching Out to THE METHODISTS with Heart and Mind

Reaching Out to THE BAPTISTS with Heart and Mind

Reaching Out to THE LUTHERANS with Heart and Mind

Reaching Out to THE EPISCOPALIANS with Heart and Mind